JUST SALMON

A beautiful cook book with the most delicious recipes that
you can prepare with the six different types of IKEA salmon.
Let yourself be inspired and enjoy all of these tasty dishes.

IKEA PRODUCT & RECIPE INDEX

SILL DILL

GRÖNSAKSKAKA

GURKA INLAGD

RÄKOR UTAN SKAL

KNÄCKEBRÖD FLERKORN

KNÄCKEBRÖD RÅG

BRÖD MJUKKAKA

KRUSTADER

LÖK ROSTAD

OST HERRGÅRD

OST PRÄST

POTATISCHIPS SALTADE

VÅFFLOR

RÄKOR MED SKAL

RÖSTI

SÅS PEPPARROT

SÅS TOMAT & ÖRT

SÅS SENAP & DILL

ÄPPELVINÄGER MED LINGON

SENAP GROV

SENAP MILD

GRATÄNG POTATIS

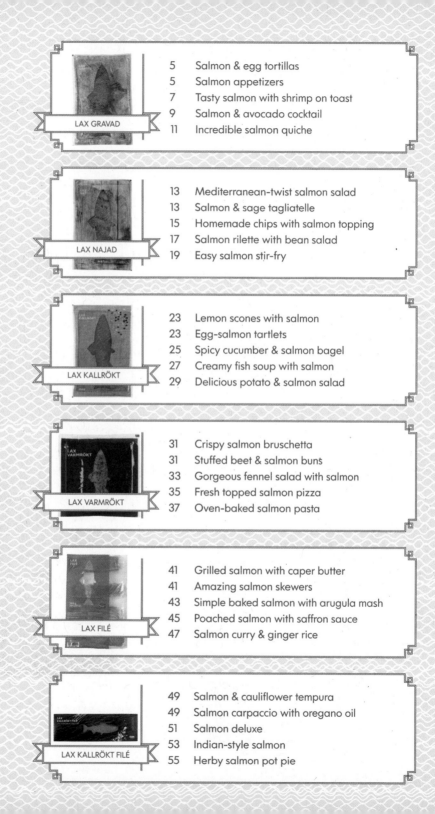

LAX GRAVAD

SALMON & EGG TORTILLAS

Breakfast dish ≈ serves 4
Preparation time ≈ approx. 10 minutes + defrosting

Ingredients ≈ ½ package (± 3.5 oz) marinated salmon LAX GRAVAD (frozen), 1 small bunch of chives, 6 eggs, 2 tablespoons heavy cream or milk, 1 tablespoon tomato ketchup, salt and pepper (freshly ground), butter for frying, 4 small flour tortillas

Defrost the marinated salmon. Finely chop the chives. Beat the eggs, cream or milk and the tomato ketchup in a bowl. Add some chopped chives and season with salt and pepper. Mix the egg mixture some more. Heat a pat of butter in a frying pan. Pour in the egg mixture and then turn down the heat. Slowly stir the eggs using a spatula until they are nearly firm.

Lay out the tortillas on plates. Divide the scrambled eggs evenly, adding them to one side of each tortilla, then season with some more salt and pepper and perhaps some chopped chives. Lay the slices of salmon on top, close the tortillas and serve.

SALMON APPETIZERS

Snack and appetizer ≈ makes ± 16 pieces
Preparation time ≈ approx. 10 minutes
+ 15 minutes baking + defrosting

Ingredients ≈ 7.1 oz marinated salmon LAX GRAVAD (frozen), 1 sheet (± 9 oz) ready made puff pastry (refrigerated or frozen), olive oil for frying, 1 clove of garlic, 10 oz fresh spinach (washed), 2.75 oz fresh cream cheese, 2 tablespoons basil pesto, salt and pepper (freshly ground), 1 egg yolk, 1 tablespoon milk, ± 1 tablespoon white sesame seeds, salmon sauce with dill SÅS SENAP & DILL
Extra ≈ parchment paper

Defrost the marinated salmon and the frozen puff pastry. Preheat the oven to 400 °F. Heat a small amount of oil in a frying pan. Peel and press the garlic into the frying pan and then add the spinach. Fry for about 2 minutes until the leaves have wilted. Scoop the spinach into a colander and let it drain (press or squeeze out the moisture).

Stir the cream cheese and pesto together and season with salt and pepper. Roll out the puff pastry and then cut it in half. Spread the cream cheese mixture over both halves. On top of this, spread out the salmon and then the spinach, then roll up the pastry. Beat together the egg yolk and the milk and brush the resulting mixture over the pastry rolls. Sprinkle the rolls with the sesame seeds and cut them into 1-inch slices. Cover a baking tray with parchment paper and lay out the slices onto it. Bake them in the oven for about 15 minutes until crispy and golden brown. Spoon some salmon sauce into a small bowl and place it on a platter. Lay out the salmon appetizers next to the sauce and serve warm (cool is also fine).

TASTY SALMON WITH SHRIMP ON TOAST

The combination of briny salmon and zesty shrimp is delightful.

Lunch and appetizer ≈ serves 4
Preparation time ≈ approx. 10 minutes + defrosting

Ingredients ≈ ½ package (± 3.5 oz) marinated salmon LAX GRAVAD (frozen), 8.8 oz peeled shrimp
RÄKOR UTAN SKAL (frozen), 2 lemons, 1 small bunch of (flat-leaf) parsley, 2 green onions,
olive oil, salt and pepper (freshly ground), 4-8 slices (sourdough) bread
Extra ≈ toaster

Defrost the marinated salmon and the shrimp. Grate the zest from 1 lemon and then juice it. Cut the other lemon into segments. Finely chop the parsley, keeping a few sprigs for garnish. Clean the green onions and cut them into thin slices. Mix together the shrimp, lemon rind, parsley and green onion with a drizzle of olive oil and then season with salt and pepper and lemon juice.

Toast the slices of bread in the toaster. Place them on the plates and divide the salmon on top. Scoop a generous spoonful of lemon shrimp onto each salmon toast. Garnish with a sprig of parsley and serve with the lemon segments.

SALMON & AVOCADO COCKTAIL

Surprise your guests with this delicious appetizer! It looks really festive served in a pretty glass.

Appetizer ≈ serves 4
Preparation time ≈ approx. 15 minutes + defrosting

Ingredients ≈ 7.1 oz marinated salmon LAX GRAVAD (frozen), ½ lemon, 3 tablespoons horseradish sauce SÅS PEPPAROT, 3 tablespoons tomato sauce (carton or canned), 1 teaspoon Worcestershire sauce, paprika, salt and pepper (freshly ground), 1 red onion, 3 avocados, 1 small bunch of celery leaves

---

Defrost the marinated salmon. Juice the half lemon. Mix the horseradish sauce, tomato sauce and Worcestershire sauce together in a bowl. Add lemon juice, paprika and salt and pepper to taste. Stir the sauce again and set aside for later use (the sauce can also be made earlier and stored in the fridge).

Peel and chop the red onion. Cut the avocados lengthways around their stones. Pull apart and remove stones. Cut the avocado halves into 3 segments, remove the skin and cut the segments into small pieces. Put the pieces of avocado in a bowl and sprinkle with some lemon juice. Cut the slices of salmon into pieces, finely chop the celery leaves and add them to the avocado, along with the chopped onion. Carefully toss the salad. Divide the salad between 4 (cocktail) glasses. Spoon on a generous scoop of sauce. Garnish with a celery leaf or some paprika, if you like. Serve the salmon and avocado cocktail. It's delicious with toast or crusty bread.

TIP

Use the rest of the carton/can of tomato sauce the day after for pasta sauce or tomato soup. Instead of tomato sauce, you could use tomato ketchup. This would make the sauce a bit sweeter.

INCREDIBLE SALMON QUICHE

Quiche is typically a dish that is just as delicious served warm as served cold.
It can therefore be prepared well in advance.

Lunch and main course ≈ serves 4-6
Preparation time ≈ approx. 15 minutes + 25 minutes baking + defrosting

---

Ingredients ≈ 7.1 oz marinated salmon LAX GRAVAD (frozen), 1 sheet (± 9 oz) ready made puff pastry
(refrigerated or frozen), 12 oz green asparagus, 2 shallots, 1 small bunch of dill,
½ piece (± 5.3 oz) of semi hard Swedish cheese OST PRÄST, butter to grease the pie plate,
4 eggs, 1 cup heavy cream, salt and pepper (freshly ground)
Extra ≈ grater STRÅLANDE or CHOSIGT, shallow pie plate or quiche form ø 11-inch SMARTA

Defrost the marinated salmon and the frozen puff pastry dough. Preheat the oven to 400 °F. Cut off the hard end of the asparagus and slice into 1/2-inch pieces. Blanch the asparagus pieces in boiling water for 3 minutes. Drain the asparagus, rinse them under a cold tap and let them drain in a colander. Peel and chop the shallots. Finely chop the dill and grate the cheese. Cut the salmon slices into thin strips. Mix the asparagus, shallots, dill, cheese and salmon together for the quiche filling.

Grease the pie plate with butter. Unroll the puff pastry dough. If the dough is too small for the plate, roll it out using a rolling pin. Line the inside of the pie plate with the dough, trim away any excess dough and spread out the filling. Beat the eggs and cream in a bowl and add salt and pepper to taste. Pour the egg-cream mixture over the salmon filling. Bake the quiche in the oven for about 25 minutes until it is firm and golden brown. Cut the hearty pastry into wedges and serve. If you are having the quiche as a main course, try serving it with a fresh green salad.

TIP

Salmon quiche is also delicious with other vegetables, such as peas, leeks, green cabbage, zucchini, watercress or cherry tomatoes.

LAX NAJAD

MEDITERRANEAN-TWIST SALMON SALAD

Appetizer ≈ serves 4-6
Preparation time ≈ approx. 15 minutes
+ 30 minutes marinating + defrosting

Ingredients ≈ 7.1 oz marinated smoked salmon
LAX NAJAD (frozen), 17.6 oz shrimp with shell
RÄKOR MED SKAL (frozen), olive oil for frying,
2 cloves garlic, ± 7 oz roasted red bell peppers (jar),
2 tablespoons mayonnaise, 1 tablespoon (Greek)
yogurt, 1 tablespoon (white) balsamic vinegar,
salt and pepper (freshly ground), 4 stalks celery,
7.5 oz artichoke hearts (jar or can), 8 sun-dried
tomatoes, 1 small bunch of basil
Extra ≈ hand blender

Thaw out the salmon and the shrimp. Add a dash of olive oil in a bowl. Peel and chop the garlic cloves fine and mix them in the oil. Peel the shrimp and stir them through the garlic oil. let and let them marinate for 30 minutes. While the shrimp are marinating, prepare the dressing. Remove the roasted skin from the bell pepper and add the pieces to the mixing beaker. Add the mayonnaise, yogurt and balsamic vinegar and purée with the hand blender until the dressing is smooth. Add salt and pepper to taste and put aside until the rest is finished.

Clean the celery stalks, remove the strings and cut into thin slices. Drain the artichokes and cut them in halves. Cut the tomatoes into thin slices and chop the salmon. Finely chop the fresh basil. Heat a frying pan and sauté the shrimp at high heat until they are warm. Remove the shrimp from the pan and let them dry on a paper towel. Mix all of the ingredients and the dressing in a bowl. Portion the salad on 4-6 small plates, sprinkle with salt and pepper and serve.

SALMON & SAGE TAGLIATELLE

Main course ≈ serves 4
Preparation time ≈ approx. 15 minutes + defrosting

Ingredients ≈ 7.1 oz marinated smoked salmon
LAX NAJAD (frozen), ± 12 oz tagliatelle,
2 tablespoons pine nuts, ⅓ piece (± 3.5 oz) of
semi hard Swedish cheese OST HERRGÅRD,
2 sticks salted butter, 1 bunch of sage, 5 oz arugula,
salt and pepper (freshly ground)
Extra ≈ grater STRÅLANDE or CHOSIGT

Defrost the salmon. Boil the tagliatelle in water with salt al dente according to the directions on the package. Cut the salmon into strips. In a dry frying pan, toast the pine nuts until they are golden brown. Remove them from the pan and let cool. Grate the cheese. Add the butter to a small pan with a thick bottom. Melt the butter until it just begins to turn light brown. Chop the sage fine and add it to the melted butter. Let them simmer for a bit and then turn off the burner. Drain the pasta, mix the salmon and arugula through it and serve on 4 pasta dishes. Drizzle the sage butter over the pasta and sprinkle with pine nuts and grated cheese. Add salt and pepper to taste and serve.

HOMEMADE CHIPS WITH SALMON TOPPING

It's fun to make your own chips, and it's much easier than you might think!
Your guests will certainly be pleased to taste such delicious chips.

Snack ≈ serves 4
Preparation time ≈ approx. 20 minutes + defrosting

Ingredients ≈ ½ package (± 3.5 oz) marinated smoked salmon LAX NAJAD (frozen), oil for deep frying,
2-3 large slightly floury potatoes, salt and pepper (freshly ground), 1 small bunch of cilantro,
1 small bunch of mint, 2-3 tablespoons sour cream, ± 3 teaspoons black lumpfish caviar
Extra ≈ deep fryer, mandoline or grater IDEALISK

Defrost the salmon. Preheat the oil in the deep fryer to 350 °F. Wash the potatoes thoroughly, but do not peel them. Cut them into 1 mm thin slices using the mandoline or grater. Do not slice them too thin or they will break. If you slice them too thick, they will not fry evenly and will turn out soggy, not crisp. Rinse the potato slices with cold water and pat them dry with a kitchen towel. Fry the chips in the hot oil a few at a time until they are golden brown. Scoop them out of the frying oil using a skimmer, place them on paper towels and sprinkle them with salt. Continue until all of the chips are done and let them cool.

Finely chop the cilantro and mint leaves. Stir the sour cream in a separate bowl. Mix in the chopped herbs and add pepper to taste. Cut the salmon into small pieces. Using a teaspoon, place a dollop of the herb-sour cream mixture on each potato chip. Place a piece of salmon on top, then garnish with a bit of the caviar. Serve the chips on an attractive large platter.

TIP

No time to make your own potato chips? The delicious salted potato chips POTATISCHIPS SALTADE are an excellent alternative!

SALMON RILLETTE WITH BEAN SALAD

This classic (traditionally prepared with meat) is suitable for any occasion.
On crackers with a beverage, in the picnic basket or as an appetizer for a dinner.

Snack, lunch and appetizer ≈ serves 4-6
Preparation time ≈ approx. 25 minutes + defrosting

Ingredients ≈ 7.1 oz marinated smoked salmon LAX NAJAD (frozen), 1 salmon filet LAX FILÉ (frozen),
3.5 oz yellow wax beans, 3.5 oz green beans, 4 tablespoons sliced pickled gherkins GURKA INLAGD,
1 small bunch of chives, 2 tablespoons mayonnaise, 2 tablespoons (Greek) yogurt, 2 tablespoons capers,
salt and pepper (freshly ground), ⅔ stick unsalted butter (softened), bread to serve
Extra ≈ food processor

Defrost the salmon. Place the salmon filet in a sauce pan and fill with water until the fish is covered. Bring the water to a boil, reduce heat and let simmer for 2 minutes, then let the salmon cool in the water. Clean the beans, then boil them for about 5 minutes until tender crisp and let them drain. Finely chop the gherkins and the chives. Stir them together with the mayonnaise, half of the yogurt, the capers and a dash of water, then season the salad dressing with salt and pepper.

Mix the butter in the food processor until it is smooth. Remove the salmon filet from the water, then pick it apart above a mixing bowl. Finely chop the smoked salmon and add it to the mixing bowl. Coarsely mix the butter, the rest of the yogurt and the salmon using the 'pulse' function. Season with salt and pepper to taste, then spoon into a bowl. Mix the beans and the dressing and serve the salad with the salmon rillette and the bread.

EASY SALMON STIR-FRY

This is a wonderful recipe that you simply must try at least once. You can vary it using different vegetables. Potatoes and salmon are very easy to combine in a recipe together.

Main course ≈ serves 4
Preparation time ≈ approx. 20 minutes + defrosting

Ingredients ≈ 7.1 oz marinated smoked salmon LAX NAJAD (frozen), 20 oz baby new potatoes (skin on),
14 oz broccoli, 8 oz snow peas, 2 red onions, 2 cloves garlic, 1 small bunch of dill,
vegetable oil for frying, salt and pepper (freshly ground), fried onion ROSTAD LÖK
Extra ≈ wok SKÄNKA, TOLERANT or IKEA 365+

Defrost the salmon. Boil the new potatoes in their skin for 10 minutes until almost done. Drain them and put them on a kitchen towel to cool. While waiting, cut the broccoli into florets and clean the snow peas. Blanch the vegetables for 4 minutes, then drain them. Peel the onions and the garlic cloves. Cut the onions in half and then into rings. Cut the garlic into thin slices. Pat the potatoes dry with the kitchen towel and then cut them in half. Cut the salmon in half lengthwise and then slice it into thin slices. Finely chop the dill.

Heat a dash of oil in the wok. Add the onions and garlic and braise lightly over low heat. Add the potato halves, increase the heat and fry them for 4 minutes, turning them until they begin to brown on all sides. Add the broccoli and the snow peas and stir-fry for 2-3 minutes until warm. Remove the heat and stir in the salmon and dill. Add salt and pepper to taste and serve on dinner plates. Sprinkle some fried onion on top and serve.

TIP

This dish can also be prepared using leftover potatoes and vegetables.

HINT OF ASIA

Salmon can be prepared in many ways. Why not try a hint of Asia? Mix together 1 teaspoon of grated ginger, ½ finely chopped red chilli pepper, 1 tablespoon of honey, 2 tablespoons of oyster sauce and 2 tablespoons of teriyaki sauce. Cover a baking tray with parchment paper and place 4 salmon fillets LAX FILÉ onto it. Generously baste them with sauce. Roast the fillets for 7-10 minutes in a pre-heated oven at 375 °F until cooked. Stir the rest of the sauce into some stir fried vegetables and serve with rice.

WITH SOME SAUCE

This starter can be made in no time. Arrange some slices of marinated smoked salmon LAX NAJAD on a plate with some salad and a tasty sauce. You can make all kinds of variations on the sauce. To make the basis of the sauce mix 2 tablespoons of mayonnaise and 2 tablespoons of sour cream together. Add various ingredients to get the desired taste: chives, dill, lemon zest, garlic, horseradish, mustard, olive tapenade, capers or paprika.

SMOKED

At IKEA we sell cold smoked salmon LAX KALLRÖKT. Salmon is smoked so that it can be preserved, and the smoking process also adds a delicious smoky taste. Unlike hot smoked salmon LAX VARMRÖKT, where the fish is smoked at a temperature between 175-200 °F, the temperatures for cold smoking do not exceed 85 °F. The duration of smoking depends on the thickness of the fish. The longer the fish is smoked the more intense the smoky taste becomes.

SUSTAINABILITY

IKEA works according to sustainable purchasing policies and only buys fish from well managed fisheries. All wild fish and seafood must come from fisheries with a MSC label (Marine Stewardship Council) or be classified as caught or raised in healthy and well managed populations by the WWF.

CHIC BREAKFAST

A chic Sunday breakfast is not complete without salmon and eggs. Using the following recipe you can serve this classic combination in an original way. Cut the top off a crusty bread roll and hollow it out so that an egg and a slice of salmon can fit inside. Spread some salmon sauce with dill SÅS SENAP & DILL on the inside of the roll and then line it with a slice of marinated salmon LAX GRAVAD. Break an egg into the roll and season with some pepper. Bake the roll for 10-12 minutes in a pre-heated oven at 350 °F until the egg has set.

HOW TO POACH

Poaching is a technique where the fish is cooked in liquid. The liquid must not boil, but should remain just below boiling point. Poached fish does not fall apart as easily and retains more flavour. Fish can be poached in salted water, stock, milk or wine. The fish can be made even more delicious by adding herbs to the poaching liquid. Thin fish fillets are cooked in about 5 minutes and thicker fillets need to be poached for 7-10 minutes. Do not throw away the poaching liquid; it is the perfect basis for sauces and soups.

ROLLED UP

Salmon is a real crowd pleaser, so it's perfect to serve at parties. Purée 3.5 oz of defrosted frozen peas together with 3.5 oz of cream cheese and 1 tablespoon of horseradish sauce SÅS PEPPARROT. Spread the mixture over 2 flour tortillas, place a few slices of cold smoked salmon LAX KALLRÖKT on each tortilla and grind some pepper on top. Roll the tortillas tightly. Cut them into pieces and arrange them on a platter.

LEMON SCONES WITH SALMON
Breakfast dish ≈ serves 2-4
Preparation time ≈ approx. 15 minutes
+ 10 minutes baking + defrosting

Ingredients ≈ ½ package (± 3.5 oz) cold smoked salmon LAX KALLRÖKT (frozen), 1 lemon, 2.4 cup all-purpose flour + extra for dusting, 1 teaspoon baking powder, ½ teaspoon salt, 2 tablespoons (cane) sugar, 0.7 stick unsalted butter (cold), 2 eggs, 4.3 fl oz milk, poppy seeds, ± 3 tablespoons clotted cream or sour cream
Extra ≈ rolling pin MAGASIN, ø 2/3-inch round pastry cutter DRÖMMAR, parchment paper

Defrost the salmon and preheat the oven to 470 °F. Grate the lemon zest. Mix the flour, baking powder, salt, sugar and lemon zest in a mixing bowl. Cut the butter into squares and mix it through the dry ingredients with your fingers until you get a crumbly texture. Beat 1 egg and milk in a separate bowl. Pour the egg and milk mixture into the other ingredients and knead into a stiff dough. Dust a clean surface with flour. Place the dough on the flour and roll it to a thickness of 1-inch. Cut circles from the dough using the pastry cutter, then place them on a baking tray covered with parchment paper. Beat the other egg separately, then glaze the dough circles and sprinkle with poppy seeds. Bake the scones in the middle of the oven for about 10 minutes until they are done and golden brown. Let the lemon scones cool, then serve together with the salmon slices and the thick cream.

Instead of the homemade scones you could also heat a few delicious waffles VÅFFLOR in the oven.

EGG-SALMON TARTLETS
Snack ≈ makes 26
Preparation time ≈ approx. 20 minutes + defrosting

Ingredients ≈ ½ package (± 3.5 oz) cold smoked salmon LAX KALLRÖKT (frozen), 5 large eggs, 1 small bunch of chervil, 1-2 tablespoons mayonnaise, 1-2 tablespoons sour cream, ½ tablespoon mild mustard SENAP MILD, salt and pepper (freshly ground), 1 box (26-piece) mini croustades KRUSTADER
Extra ≈ food processor, piping bag with star tip (medium)

Defrost the salmon. Hard-boil the eggs for about 7 minutes. Rinse them in cold water and let them cool. Keep a few sprigs of chervil separate for the garnish. Finely chop the rest of the chervil sprigs. Cut the salmon in small pieces. Peel the eggs and put them in the food processor. Add half of the salmon, the mayonnaise, sour cream and mustard to the eggs and mix until smooth. Remove the cutter from the food processor and mix in the rest of the salmon and chervil. Add salt and pepper to taste and fill the piping bag with the mixture. Fill the mini croustades with attractive rosettes of the egg-salmon mixture. Garnish with a chervil leaf and serve on a large platter or tray.

No time to cook? Fill the mini croustades with a little bit of sour cream and a piece of marinated herring with dill SILL DILL.

SPICY CUCUMBER & SALMON BAGEL

Sweet, sour, salty and spicy. The combination of these tastes makes for a surprising sandwich.

Lunch ≈ serves 4
Preparation time ≈ approx. 10 minutes + defrosting

Ingredients ≈ 7.1 oz cold smoked salmon LAX KALLRÖKT (frozen), 1 lime, 1 piece (± 2-inch) of ginger, 2 tablespoons vegetable oil, 1 teaspoon sesame oil, ½ tablespoon honey, salt and pepper (freshly ground), ½-1 cucumber, 1 red chilli pepper, 2 green onions, ± 2 oz fresh bean sprouts, 4 (sesame) bagels

Defrost the salmon. Juice the lime. Peel and grate the ginger. For the dressing, stir the olive oil, sesame oil, honey and ginger together in a bowl. Add the lime juice and salt and pepper to taste. Cut the cucumber in half lengthways. Remove the seeds from the cucumber with a spoon and cut it into slices. Cut the chilli pepper in half lengthways. Remove the seeds and cut the chilli into thin strips. Clean the green onions and cut them into small rings. Mix the cucumber, chilli, green onion rings, bean sprouts and the dressing together in a bowl.

Slice the bagels. Place the bottom halves on plates and top them with slices of smoked salmon. Spoon on the spicy cucumber salad. Cover with the top halves of the bagels and serve.

TIP

Make the salad into a whole meal. To do this boil ± 11 oz noodles, cool them off in cold water and then drain them. Mix the noodles, the cucumber salad and the salmon together.

CREAMY FISH SOUP WITH SALMON

A hearty soup with fish and vegetables that you can serve all year round.

Lunch and appetizer ≈ serves 4
Preparation time ≈ approx. 35 minutes + defrosting

Ingredients ≈ ½ package (± 3.5 oz) cold smoked salmon LAX KALLRÖKT (frozen), 4 slices of soft wheat bread BRÖD MJUKKAKA (frozen), 2 onions, 1 large carrot, 1 fennel bulb, olive oil for frying, 1 bay leaf, 11 fl oz fish stock, 3.5 fl oz dry white wine, 14 oz cod fillet, ½ stick unsalted butter, 0.4 cup all-purpose flour, 0.5 cup heavy cream, salt and pepper (freshly ground), 1 small bunch of (flat-leaf) parsley

Defrost the salmon and the bread. Peel and chop the onions. Clean the carrot and cut it into thin slices. Clean the fennel bulb, cut it in half lengthways and then into slices. Heat a small amount of oil in a large saucepan, add the onion, carrot, fennel and bay leaf and sweat on a low heat for 5 minutes. Add the stock and the wine and let simmer for 15 minutes. In the meantime, cut the cod into pieces.

Pour the stock through a sieve, keeping the liquid and the vegetables but removing the bay leaf. Melt the butter in the pan. Add the flour, stir it into the butter and let it cook. Slowly pour in the stock while stirring constantly with a whisk. Add the pieces of cod and the vegetables and heat the soup for a further 4 minutes. Stir in the cream and season the soup with salt and pepper. Cut the smoked salmon into pieces, finely chop the parsley and cut the bread into thick slices. Pour the soup into the bowls. Add the salmon to the soup, then sprinkle some parsley and pepper on top. Serve with the bread.

TIP

Try replacing half of the cod with salmon fillets LAX FILÉ and adding 4 oz peeled shrimp RÄKOR UTAN SKAL to the soup along with the smoked salmon.

DELICIOUS POTATO & SALMON SALAD

A wonderful salad with tasty ingredients. The vinegar gives it a pleasantly crisp taste.

Lunch and appetizer ≈ serves 4
Preparation time ≈ approx. 25 minutes + defrosting

Ingredients ≈ 7.1 oz cold smoked salmon LAX KALLRÖKT (frozen), 17 oz waxy potatoes,
2-3 tablespoons mayonnaise or yogurt, 1-2 tablespoons white wine vinegar or apple vinegar
with lingonberries ÄPPELVINÄGER MED LINGON, 1 small bunch of chives,
salt and pepper (freshly ground), 1 bunch of radishes, ± 4 oz black olives (pitted),
2 eggs, 6 oz dandelion salad or fresh spinach (washed), bread to serve (optional)
Extra ≈ steamer insert STABIL

Defrost the salmon. Wash the potatoes with the skins on, then cut them into evenly-sized pieces. Place the steamer insert in a pan with boiling water, then add the potatoes. Place the lid on the pan and let the potatoes steam for about 12 minutes until done. Remove the insert from the pan and let the potatoes cool. While the potatoes are cooling, prepare the dressing. Finely chop the chives. Mix the mayonnaise or yogurt and the vinegar together in a mixing bowl. Add the chopped chives, stir and add salt and pepper to taste. Clean the radishes and cut them into thin slices. Drain the olives. Boil the eggs for 5-6 minutes until soft boiled, rinse them with cold water and remove the shells.

Carefully toss the potatoes, radish slices, dandelion salad or spinach leaves, olives and dressing in a salad bowl. Place the slices of salmon on one side of the plates, then serve the potato salad on the other. Cut the soft-boiled eggs in half and place them on the salad. Add salt and pepper to taste, then serve with bread, if you like.

LAX VARMRÖKT

CRISPY SALMON BRUSCHETTA

Snack ≈ makes 20
Preparation time ≈ approx. 15 minutes
+ 10 minutes baking + defrosting

Ingredients ≈ 14.1 oz hot smoked salmon
LAX VARMRÖKT (frozen), 1 baguette,
olive oil for frying, 1 clove of garlic, 1 zucchini,
Herbs de Provence, salt and pepper
(freshly ground), 1 small bunch of basil
Extra ≈ parchment paper, grill pan GRILLA

Defrost the salmon. Preheat the oven to 400 °F.
Cut the baguette into 20 thin slices and lay these
onto parchment paper on a baking tray. Pour a
small amount of olive oil into a bowl. Peel and press
the garlic into the bowl, mix, and brush the bread
with the mixture (this is best done with a basting
brush). Bake the slices of bread in the oven for about
10 minutes until they are lightly browned and crispy.
Remove them from the oven and let them cool.

In the meantime, wash and dry the zucchini and cut
it into 3 pieces. Then cut these pieces into thin slices
lengthways. Lightly brush the slices with oil and
season them with Herbs de Provence, salt and pepper.
Heat the grill pan and grill the zucchini on both sides
until the slices have nice light brown grill stripes on
both sides. Place a slice of grilled zucchini on each
piece of baguette. Separate the salmon into pieces,
using a fork, and coarsely chop the fresh basil. Evenly
distribute the pieces of salmon onto the zucchini and
garnish with the basil. Place the bruschetta on a platter
and serve.

STUFFED BEET & SALMON BUNS

Lunch ≈ serves 4
Preparation time ≈ approx. 10 minutes + defrosting

Ingredients ≈ 14.1 oz hot smoked salmon
LAX VARMRÖKT (frozen), ± 8 oz cooked red beets,
2 shallots, 1 small bunch of dill,
2 tablespoons (Greek) yogurt, salt and pepper
(freshly ground), 8 hot dog buns, 2-3 oz arugula

Defrost the salmon. Clean the beets and cut them
into small cubes. Peel and chop the shallots. Finely
chop the dill. Mix together the beetroot pieces, the
chopped shallots, the dill and the yogurt and season
the resulting salad with salt and pepper. Coarsely chop
the arugula. Separate the salmon into pieces using a
fork. Open the buns and put 2 on each plate. Put some
arugula in the buns, then spoon in the beet salad and
the salmon pieces.

TIP

Try putting the salad and salmon on crunchy crackers.
Multigrain crispbread KNÄCKEBRÖD FLERKORN or
rye crispbread KNÄCKEBRÖD RÅG from IKEA are
perfect for this.

GORGEOUS FENNEL SALAD WITH SALMON

The oranges and the salmon complement one another well in this colourful salad.

Salad and appetizer ≈ serves 4
Preparation time ≈ approx. 15 minutes + defrosting

Ingredients ≈ 14.1 oz hot smoked salmon LAX VARMRÖKT (frozen), 2 oranges, 1 tablespoon whole-grain mustard SENAP GROV, 2 tablespoons olive oil, 1 tablespoon white wine vinegar, salt and pepper (freshly ground), 1 fennel bulb, 1 cucumber, 1 red onion, ± 7 oz cannellini beans (canned), 3.5 oz mixed salad
Extra ≈ mandoline or grater IDEALISK

Defrost the salmon and pick it apart with a fork. Cut off the orange peels, exposing the flesh. Cut the oranges into wedges between the membranes over a bowl to catch the juice. For the dressing, stir the mustard, oil, vinegar and the juice from the orange together in the bowl. Season with salt and pepper to taste. Clean the fennel bulb and cut it into thin slices. Slice the cucumber with the mandoline or grater into strips lengthwise. Peel the onion, cut it in half and then slice it into rings. Rinse the beans and let them dry in a strainer. Mix all of the ingredients (except for the salmon) with the dressing in a mixing bowl. Spoon the salad into a large serving dish and spread the salmon on top. Enjoy with bread and butter.

TIP

You can replace the beans with peas, fava beans, green asparagus or green beans. Or add all of them together for a hearty dinner salad.

FRESH TOPPED SALMON PIZZA

Pizza made from scratch tastes so much better. Serve as a snack with a beverage or as a main course with a healthy side salad.

Snack, lunch and main course ≈ serves 2-4
Preparation time ≈ approx. 10 minutes + 12 minutes baking + defrosting

---

Ingredients ≈ 14.1 oz hot smoked salmon LAX VARMRÖKT (frozen), olive oil for frying, 1 glove of garlic,
± 17 oz fresh spinach (washed), 8 oz fresh mozzarella, 2 ready-made pizza crusts or pizza dough,
½ cup prepared tomato sauce, 2 tablespoons capers, ½ tablespoon dried oregano, pinch of chilli powder
Extra ≈ parchment paper, rolling pin MAGASIN (if using pizza dough)

Defrost the salmon and pick it apart with a fork. Preheat the oven to 400 °F. Heat a dash of oil in a frying pan. Peel the garlic and press the clove out above the pan. Add the spinach and stir-fry until it begins to wilt. Move the spinach to a colander and let it drain. Cut or pick the mozzarella into pieces.

Place a sheet of parchment paper on a baking tray and lay the pizza crusts on the paper. If you are using pizza dough, roll it out onto the parchment paper using the rolling pin. In the following order, spread the tomato sauce, spinach, salmon, mozzarella and capers over the pizza crusts. Sprinkle with oregano and chilli powder and drizzle a bit of oil on top. Bake the pizzas for 12-15 minutes in the oven until they are hot and the crusts are golden brown.

TIP

You can also make the tomato sauce from scratch. Cut 17 oz tomatoes in half, then place them in a roasting pan with 2 peeled cloves of garlic. Pour a bit of olive oil in the pan and sprinkle with pepper and salt. Roast the tomatoes at 400 °F for 20 minutes. Purée the roasted tomatoes with a hand blender and you have your own homemade tomato sauce.

OVEN-BAKED SALMON PASTA

The ready-to-eat tomato and herb sauce is delightfully creamy. Once in the oven, it smells so delicious that you almost don't want to wait for it to finish baking.

Main course ≈ serves 4
Preparation time ≈ approx. 15 minutes + 15 minutes baking + defrosting

---

Ingredients ≈ 14.1 oz hot smoked salmon LAX VARMRÖKT (frozen), 11 oz pasta (rigatoni or penne),
1 large onion, 1 eggplant, olive oil for frying, 3 tablespoons pine nuts, 14 oz mixed cherry tomatoes,
½ piece (± 5.3 oz) of semi hard Swedish cheese OST HERRGÅRD, 1 bag (9 oz) tomato and herb sauce
SÅS TOMAT & ÖRT, salt and pepper (freshly ground), 1 small bunch of basil
Extra ≈ grater STRÅLANDE or GHOSIGT, oven dish VITLING, MIXTUR or SMARTA

Defrost the salmon. Preheat the oven to 400 °F. Boil the pasta in water with salt until al dente according to the directions on the package. While the pasta is boiling, peel and finely chop the onion and dice the eggplant. Heat a dash of oil in a frying pan and soften the onions for 3 minutes over low heat. Add the eggplant and braise for another 3 minutes. Heat another dry frying pan and toast the pine nuts until light brown. Cut the cherry tomatoes in half and grate the cheese. Pick the salmon apart using a fork.

Drain the pasta and mix it together with the eggplant and onion. Add the salmon, pine nuts, tomatoes and tomato sauce and mix the ingredients together. Season with salt and pepper to taste. Spoon the pasta into an oven dish and sprinkle with the grated cheese. Bake the pasta dish in the oven for about 15 minutes until golden brown. Coarsely chop the fresh basil. Remove the dish from the oven, garnish with the basil and serve.

FANTASTIC STEW

Salmon is a perfect ingredient for stews. Mix 1 clove of garlic, roughly chopped, 1 teaspoon ground cilantro, 1 tablespoon ginger syrup, 3 tablespoons soy sauce and 3 tablespoons fish sauce together. Place 4 salmon filets LAX FILÉ in a deep plate, pour the marinade over it, cover and let sit in the refrigerator for at least 2 hours. Heat a dash of vegetable oil in a wok. Add 1 clove of garlic chopped, the marinated salmon and a diced half pineapple. Cover in fish bouillon. Bring to a boil and let simmer for 25-30 minutes. Stir the salmon occasionally. The stew is done when the liquid has almost completely vaporated.

SALMON SANDWICH

Salmon sandwiches are delicious and everyone enjoys them. Toast 2 slices of sandwich bread (white or wheat). Stir-fry ± 5 oz fresh spinach (washed) in a small amount of olive oil until the leaves begin to wilt. Put the spinach in a sieve and let it drain. Next, chop the spinach, mix it with 2 oz soft goat's cheese and 1 tablespoon of mild mustard SENAP MILD. Spread the mixture on one slice of bread, then cover it with 2 slices of marinated smoked salmon LAX NAJAD. Top it off with the other slice of bread, cut diagonally and serve.

DIGGING A HOLE

IKEA sells the popular marinated salmon LAX GRAVAD. This is a typical Scandinavian dish that is traditionally eaten with a sweet mustard and dill sauce. The name is derived from the method that medieval fishermen used to preserve their catch. The salmon was salted and then buried in the ground to allow it to ripen. 'Grav' is the Swedish word for 'hole in the ground', and 'lax' means 'salmon'.

TRULY HEALTHY

Salmon is a fatty fish, and fat in fish is very healthy. Omega-3 fatty acids play a vital role in preventing cardiovascular diseases. 3.5 oz of salmon contain around 0.11 oz of omega-3, which is coincidentally the recommended daily allowance. Salmon is also a good source of the minerals iodine (good for metabolism), selenium (which prevents the formation of harmful substances in the body) and vitamin D (important for strong bones, teeth and immune system).

SALMON NIÇOISE

Salad Niçoise is traditionally made with tuna, but salmon is a delicious variation on the recipe. For the dressing, mix 1 tablespoon of whole-grain mustard SENAP GROV, 1-2 tablespoons white wine vinegar, 2-3 tablespoons olive oil and salt and pepper to taste. Use a fork to pick the hot smoked salmon LAX VARMRÖKT apart into small pieces. In a salad bowl, mix together 6 oz boiled new potatoes, 6 oz blanched green beans, 7 oz mixed salad, 2 oz Kalamata olives, 4 diced tomatoes, the salmon and the dressing. Serve topped with 2 halved soft-boiled eggs.

PLEASANTLY PINK

The meat of salmon can vary in colour from pink and orange to deep red. Salmon is actually a whitefish, but their diet of shrimp and crabs can change the colour of their meat. Shrimp and crabs eat algae and seaweed that contain a red pigment. This pigment is stored in their shells and in their tissue. When the salmon eat them, the red pigment is then stored in the salmon's fat. Not all salmon have the same diet, so they display a wide range of colours in nature. Farmed salmon obtains its colour from its food as well.

FRYING SALMON IS EASY

It may seem difficult to fry salmon, but it is actually very simple. Place a Teflon frying pan on high heat. Glaze the salmon filets (with or without skin) or chunks with oil and season them with salt and pepper. Place the salmon (skin down) in the pan. Reduce the heat and let the salmon fry for about 3 minutes. Do not shake the pan. Carefully turn the salmon over and reduce the heat even more. Let it fry for another 2 minutes until the fish is done.

GRILLED SALMON WITH CAPER BUTTER

Main course ≈ serves 4
Preparation time ≈ approx. 20 minutes
+ 20 minutes stiffening + defrosting

Ingredients ≈ 4 salmon fillets LAX FILÉ (frozen),
1 lemon, 1 stick unsalted butter (at room temperature),
1 clove of garlic, 3 tablespoons capers,
salt and pepper (freshly ground), 22 oz broccoli,
1 box (16.9 oz) rösti RÖSTI (frozen), olive oil for frying
Extra ≈ aluminium foil, grill pan GRILLA

Defrost the salmon fillets. Grate the lemon zest. Put the butter in a bowl. Press the clove of garlic and add it. Add the lemon zest and the capers and mix well. Season with salt and pepper. Spoon the caper butter onto a piece of aluminium foil, roll it up neatly and put it in the fridge to harden for at least 20 minutes.

Preheat the oven to 375 °F. Cut the broccoli into florets. Lay out the rösti on the grate of the oven and heat them for 10 minutes. Meanwhile, boil the broccoli in salted water for about 5 minutes until al dente. Heat the grill pan. Lightly brush the salmon fillets with olive oil and season with salt and pepper. Grill the fish for 2-3 minutes on each side until just cooked. Take the Evenly portion the rösti and broccoli onto the plates. Place the grilled salmon next to it and lay a piece of caper butter onto each piece of salmon.

AMAZING SALMON SKEWERS

Main course ≈ serves 4
Preparation time ≈ approx. 20 minutes + defrosting

Ingredients ≈ 4 salmon fillets LAX FILÉ (frozen),
1 lime, 1 bunch of cilantro, 3 tablespoons (Greek)
yogurt, 1 tablespoon sweet chilli sauce, salt and
pepper (freshly ground), 9 oz button mushrooms,
1 bok choi, 9 oz noodles, vegetable oil for
frying, soy sauce, 3.5 oz cashew nuts
Extra ≈ 4 wooden skewers,
wok SKÄNKA, TOLERANT or IKEA 365+

Defrost the salmon and soak the wooden skewers in water. Grate the lime zest and squeeze out its juice. Cut each salmon fillet into 3 pieces and push the pieces onto the skewers. Drizzle lime juice over them and set them aside. Meanwhile, make the cilantro yogurt. Finely chop the cilantro and mix it with the yogurt and the chilli sauce. Season with salt and pepper. Clean the mushrooms and cut them into quarters. Roughly chop the bok choi. Cook the noodles until al dente according to the instructions on the packet and let them drain.

Sprinkle lime zest and some salt and pepper over the skewers. Heat a small amount of oil in a frying pan and fry the skewers for about 5 minutes while turning them until they are cooked on all sides. Heat a small amount of oil in the wok and stir fry the mushrooms and bok choi for 3 minutes. Add the noodles and fry for a further 2 minutes. Add soy sauce to taste and scatter the cashew nuts on top. Scoop some noodles onto the plates. Place a salmon skewer on each plate and serve with the cilantro yogurt.

SIMPLE BAKED SALMON WITH ARUGULA MASH

Meat and fish is an unusual combination, but the flavours in this dish may surprise you.

Main course ≈ serves 4
Preparation time ≈ approx. 12 minutes + 15 minutes baking + defrosting

---

Ingredients ≈ 4 salmon filets LAX FILÉ (frozen), salt and pepper (freshly ground), 1 piece (± 5 oz) salami,
1 jar (± 5 oz) dried tomatoes, 1 lemon, 1 sprig of thyme, 4 fl oz white wine,
1 package (± 14 oz) mashed potatoes, 1 pat of unsalted butter, ± 7 oz arugula
Extra ≈ oven dish LYCKAD, VITLING or IKEA 365+

Defrost the salmon. Preheat the oven to 400 °F. Place the salmon in an oven dish and season with salt and pepper. Cut the salami into very small cubes. Remove the tomatoes from the jar and save the oil for later. Finely chop the tomatoes. Grate the lemon zest. Remove the thyme leaves from the sprigs. Mix the salami, tomatoes, thyme leaves, lemon zest, white wine and the oil from the jar of dried tomatoes in a bowl and spread it over the salmon in the oven dish. Bake the salmon in the middle of the oven for about 15 minutes until done.

While the salmon is baking, prepare the mashed mashed potatoes according to the directions on the package. Add a pat of butter and season with salt and pepper to taste. Put the lid on the pan and keep the mash warm. Remove the salmon from the oven. Mix the arugula through the warm mashed potatoes. Place a salmon filet on each plate, spoon some of the tomato-salami mixture on top and serve with the arugula mash.

POACHED SALMON WITH SAFFRON SAUCE

A wonderful dish to prepare at the weekend or when you have extra time to spend in the kitchen. The saffron sauce gives the dish an attractive colour.

Main course ≈ serves 4
Preparation time ≈ approx. 25 minutes + 30 minutes baking + defrosting

---

Ingredients ≈ 4 salmon filets LAX FILÉ (frozen), butter to grease the oven dishes, ½ bag (14 oz) potatoes au gratin GRATÄNG POTATIS (frozen), 7 oz green beans, 12 carrots (with greens), 2 small leeks, 7 fl oz dry white wine, 6 saffron stems, 0.5 cup heavy cream, salt and pepper (freshly ground), ± 16 fl oz vegetable bouillon, 6 oz fava beans (shelled)
Extra ≈ 4 one-person oven dishes SMARTA

Defrost the salmon. Preheat the oven to 400 °F. Grease the oven dishes with butter and fill them with the potatoes au gratin. Place the dishes in the oven and bake the gratin for 30-35 minutes until golden brown. While the potatoes are baking, clean the green beans, the carrots (leaving a bit of the green stems) and the leeks. Cut the leeks into 1/2-inch pieces. Bring half of the wine and the saffron stems to a simmer in a sauce pan and reduce it to half of the volume. Add the cream, reduce the sauce a bit more and then season with salt and pepper to taste. Keep the sauce warm until you are ready to use it.

In the meantime, add the vegetable bouillon and the rest of the wine to a sauté pan and bring it to a simmer. Season with salt and pepper. Add the green beans and the carrots and let them simmer for 5 minutes. Add the leeks and the fava beans and cook for another 5 minutes. Carefully place the salmon in the bouillon and poach the filets for about 5 minutes until the fish is done. Divide the vegetables among 4 deep plates. Place the poached salmon on top of the vegetables and ladle a generous serving of the saffron sauce on top. Remove the potatoes au gratin from the oven and serve them with the salmon.

You can also prepare the tasty vegetable medallions GRÖNSAKSKAKA instead of the potatoes au gratin.

SALMON CURRY & GINGER RICE

Salmon with an Asian accent. Fried ginger rice is a refreshing change from the usual boiled white rice.

Main course ≈ serves 4
Preparation time ≈ approx. 30 minutes + defrosting

Ingredients ≈ 4 salmon filets LAX FILÉ (frozen), 1 onion, 2 cloves garlic, 1 piece (± 2-inch) of ginger,
8 oz sugar snap peas or snow peas, 1 yellow bell pepper, 2 cups long grain rice, vegetable oil for frying,
1 stalk lemongrass, 1-2 tablespoons red curry paste, 1 can (14 fl oz) coconut milk,
1 tablespoon fish sauce, salt and pepper (freshly ground), 1 small bunch of cilantro (optional)
Extra ≈ wok SKÄNKA, TOLERANT or IKEA 365+

Defrost the salmon and cut it in pieces. Peel the onion and the garlic. Chop the onion and cut the garlic into thin slices. Peel and grate the ginger. Clean the sugar snap peas or snow peas. Clean the bell pepper and cut it into thin slices. Boil the rice according to the directions on the package and drain. Heat a dash of oil in the wok and soften the onions for 2 minutes over low heat. Bruise the lemongrass, add it and the curry paste to the wok and simmer for 1 minute. Add the coconut milk. Add the bell pepper strips and the sugar snaps or snow peas and simmer over medium heat for 10 minutes. Stir in the salmon and the fish sauce and simmer for another 5 minutes until the salmon is done. Season the curry with salt and pepper to taste.

Heat a dash of oil in a frying pan. Add the grated ginger and the garlic slices and let them sauté for a bit. Add the rice and stir-fry for about 2 minutes until the rice is warm. Divide the rice among 4 deep plates or bowls, then add the curry on top. Garnish with some chopped cilantro, if you like.

LAX KALLRÖKT FILÉ

SALMON & CAULIFLOWER TEMPURA

Snack and appetizer ≈ serves 4-6
Preparation time ≈ approx. 20 minutes + defrosting

Ingredients ≈ 14 oz cold smoked salmon loin
LAX KALLRÖKT FILÉ (frozen), 16-32 fl oz peanut oil,
1 cauliflower, 2 tablespoons white sesame seeds,
3 tablespoons soy sauce, 1 tablespoon sesame oil,
1 egg, ± 6.8 fl oz ice-cold water, 1 cup all-purpose
flour, salt and pepper (freshly ground)
Extra ≈ wok SKÄNKA, TOLERANT or IKEA 365+

Defrost the salmon. Heat the peanut oil in the wok.
While waiting, cut the salmon into thin slices. Cut
the cauliflower into small florets. Toast the sesame
seeds in a dry frying pan until they begin to brown.
To make the dip, stir the sesame seeds, soy sauce
and sesame oil together in a bowl. Beat the egg in a
mixing bowl. Beat the ice-cold water into the beaten
egg. Sift the flower into the mixture, add pepper and
salt to taste and continue mixing (don't worry - it's
OK to leave some lumps in the mixture). Use a small
piece of bread to test whether the oil is hot enough.
You can tell if the bread begins to simmer. Dip the
salmon and cauliflower in the batter and fry them in
the oil in small portions for about 2 minutes until they
are golden brown. Let the portions drip dry on a bed
of paper towels. Serve the tempura together with the
sesame soy dip.

TIP

Shrimp tempura is also very tasty. Defrost and peel
the shrimp with shell RÄKOR MED SKAL and add
1 teaspoon of curry powder to the tempura batter.

SALMON CARPACCIO WITH OREGANO OIL

Lunch and appetizer ≈ serves 4
Preparation time ≈ approx. 15 minutes + defrosting

Ingredients ≈ 14 oz cold smoked salmon loin
LAX KALLRÖKT FILÉ (frozen), 1 lemon, 1 small bunch
of oregano, 4 tablespoons olive oil, 1 shallot,
1-2 oz watercress, salt and pepper (freshly ground)
Extra ≈ mortar and pestel ÄDELSTEN

Allow the salmon to defrost a bit (but not completely,
because that would make it more difficult to slice).
Cut the salmon into thin slices and portion them
on the plates. Cut the lemon in half. Press the juice
from one half and cut the other into wedges. Grind
the oregano fine using the mortar and pestel. Stir in
the oil and add lemon juice to taste. Peel the shallot,
cut it into thin slices and separate the rings. Sprinkle
the cress and shallot rings over the salmon carpaccio
and drizzle with oregano oil. Season with some salt
and pepper and serve with a lemon wedge.

SALMON DELUXE

This is an excellent dish to serve when you have company. You can portion the salmon loin at the table and your guests can choose their own garnishes.

Appetizer ≈ serves 4
Preparation time ≈ approx. 20 minutes + approx. 2 hours freezing + defrosting

Ingredients ≈ 14 oz cold smoked salmon loin LAX KALLRÖKT FILÉ (frozen), ice cubes, 1 cup heavy cream, 1 tablespoon horseradish, 1 egg, 2 shallots, 4 tablespoons sliced pickled gherkins GURKA INLAGD, 2 tablespoons capers, 1 small bunch of chives, 2 tablespoons sour cream, 2 tablespoons salmon sauce with dill SÅS SENAP & DILL
Extra ≈ hand mixer or hand blender, freezer food container, ice-cream scoop CHOSIGT

While the salmon is defrosting, prepare the horseradish ice cream. Place a bowl inside another bowl filled with ice cubes and cold water. Pour the cream into the inner bowl and stir in the horseradish. Using a hand mixer or hand blender, blend until the mixture is as thick as custard. Spoon the mixture into the food container and place it in the freezer for about 2 hours until thoroughly frozen.

Boil the egg for 7 minutes in boiling water and rinse it off in cold water. Peel the egg, chop it fine and place it in a small dish. Peel and finely chop the shallots and add them to another small dish. Finely chop the gherkin slices and the capers and put them in separate small dishes. Finely chop the chives and stir it into the sour cream. Place this mixture into a bowl. Spoon the salmon sauce into another bowl.

Place a small spoon in each of the bowls and dishes and put them on the table. Place the salmon on a cutting board. Remove the horseradish ice cream from the freezer. Serve a scoop of ice cream on each plate and serve immediately. Cut the salmon into nice thin slices at the table and serve it on the plates. Let your guests garnish their salmon as they wish with the various garnishes and sauces.

INDIAN-STYLE SALMON

*An Indian salmon variation. The spicy lentils and
the crisp mint give the dish a delicious flavour.*

Main course ≈ serves 4
Preparation time ≈ approx. 30 minutes + 10 minutes baking + defrosting

---

Ingredients ≈ ± 26 oz cold smoked salmon loin LAX KALLRÖKT FILÉ (frozen), 1 cup French lentils,
1 red chilli pepper, 1 red bell pepper, 1 eggplant, 3 green onions, vegetable oil for frying,
2 tablespoons curry powder, 2 naan breads, 1 sprig of mint and/or (flat-leaf) parsley
Extra ≈ parchment paper, toaster

Defrost the salmon. Preheat the oven to 400 °F. Boil the lentils until al dente according to the directions on the package and let them drain. While the lentils are cooking, clean the peppers and cut the red chilli pepper into rings and the bell pepper into strips. Clean the eggplant and cut it into ± 1-inch cubes. Clean the green onions and cut them into rings. Cut the salmon into 4 equal pieces, then place them on a baking tray covered with parchment paper. Brush the salmon with oil and sprinkle it with half of the curry powder. Bake the salmon in the middle of the oven for about 10 minutes until heated.

In the meantime, heat a dash of oil in a large frying pan and stir-fry the peppers and eggplant for 4 minutes. Add the boiled lentils, the green onion and the rest of the curry powder and fry for another 3 minutes until the lentils are hot. Toast the naan bread in the toaster and cut it into pieces. Coarsely chop the sprigs of mint and/or parsley. Remove the salmon from the oven. Divide the lentils among the plates and portion the salmon on top of the lentils. Garnish with the chopped herbs and serve with the naan bread.

TIP

You can leave out the chilli pepper for a milder dish.

HERBY SALMON POT PIE

This is an excellent dish for the whole family. Don't let the number of ingredients intimidate you – the dish is very easy to prepare.

Main course ≈ serves 4
Preparation time ≈ approx. 25 minutes + approx. 20 minutes baking + defrosting

---

Ingredients ≈ 14 oz cold smoked salmon loin LAX KALLRÖKT FILÉ (frozen), 1 sheet (± 9 oz) ready made puff pastry (refrigerated or frozen), 2 large potatoes, 2 onions, 1 sprig of rosemary, 1 sprig of thyme, butter for frying, 4 tablespoons all-purpose flour, 1 bottle (12 fl oz) light beer, 8 oz peas (frozen), 4 tablespoons heavy cream, 2 tablespoons whole-grain mustard SENAP GROV, salt and pepper (freshly ground), 1 egg yolk
Extra ≈ rolling pin MAGASIN, oven dish SMARTA

Defrost the salmon and cut it into pieces. If you are using frozen pastry dough, let it defrost. Preheat the oven to 400 °F. Peel and dice the potatoes. Peel and chop the onions. Remove the rosemary leaves from the sprigs and chop them fine. Remove the thyme leaves from the sprigs. Heat a large pat of butter in a sauce pan and stir-fry the potatoes and onions until the potatoes begin to turn brown. Add the herbs and flour and let them sauté for a bit. Slowly add the beer while stirring until the sauce thickens. Stir in the salmon, peas, cream and mustard and season with salt and pepper to taste. Put the fish ragout in the oven dish. Beat the egg yolk. Unroll the puff pastry dough, cover the oven dish and press the edges closed. Cut a few holes in the top of the crust and brush with the beaten egg yolk. Bake the pot pie for about 20 minutes until golden brown.

TIP

Replace the beer with fish or vegetable bouillon if you would prefer not to use alcohol.

COLOPHON

IKEA Project Management
Donna Fitzgerald

Idea, execution, art direction & realisation
Wowhow B.V.

Editorial
Ellen Heintges

Recipes, text & styling
Annemieke Heintges

Translation
Taalmaat

Photography
Remko Kraaijeveld

Culinary realisation
Sander de Ponti

Design & illustrations
Kelly Verhallen

Image processing
Dinq media

Printing & technical editing
Hazenberg Hoefsloot

Paper
Printed on FSC paper

First edition 2015

Copyright © Wowhow B.V., Mierlo (the Netherlands).

For more information, visit our website: IKEA.us